Amazing Animal Hunters

ALLIGATORS
and
CROCODILES

by Sally Morgan

amicus

Published by Amicus
P.O. Box 1329, Mankato, Minnesota 56002

Printed in the United States of America at Corporate Graphics, in North Mankato, Minnesota.

Library of Congress Cataloging-in-Publication Data
Morgan, Sally.
 Alligators and crocodiles / by Sally Morgan.
    p. cm. -- (Amazing animal hunters)
 Includes index.
 ISBN 978-1-60753-043-5 (library binding)
 1. Alligators--Juvenile literature. 2. Crocodiles--Juvenile literature. I. Title.
 QL666.C925M653 2011
 597.98--dc22

                                                            2009049338

Created by Q2AMedia
Editor: Katie Dicker
Art Director: Harleen Mehta
Designer: Dibakar Acharjee
Picture Researcher: Maria Janet

All words in **bold** can be found in the Glossary on pages 30–31.

Picture credits
t=top b=bottom c=center l=left r=right
Cover images: Elizabeth DeLaney/Photolibrary, Shutterstock

James Robinson/Photolibrary: Title page, Yuriy Kulyk/Shutterstock: Contents page, Wando Studios/Istockphoto: 4, Robert Nichol/Ecoscene: 5t, Cc. Lockwood/Photolibrary: 5b, Hansjoerg Richter/Istockphoto: 6t, Shelly Perry/Istockphoto: 6b, Barry Hughes/Ecoscene: 7, Fritz Polking/Ecoscene: 9, Stan Osolinski/Photolibrary: 10, Brian Kenney/Photolibrary: 11, Franco Banfi/NHPA: 12, Henry Ausloos/Photolibrary: 13, Fritz Polking/Ecoscene: 14, Philippe Henry/Photolibrary: 15t, Fritz Polking/Ecoscene: 15b, Werner Bollmann/Photolibrary: 16, Jonathan & Angela Scott/NHPA: 17t, Fritz Poelking/ Photolibrary: 17b, Mark Deeble & Victoria Stone/Photolibrary: 18, Patricio Robles Gil/Photolibrary: 19t, Wh Chow/ Dreamstime: 19b, James Robinson/Photolibrary: 20, David M Dennis/Photolibrary: 21t, Dani/Jeske/Photolibrary: 21b, Dr Myrna Watanabe/Photolibrary: 22, Dreamstime: 23, Mario Castillo/Reuters: 24, Roger De La Harpe/Abpl/Photolibrary: 25t, Dr Myrna Watanabe/Photolibrary: 25b, Tobias Bernhard/ Photolibrary: 26, JTB Photo/Photolibrary: 27, Wayne Lawler/Ecoscene: 28, Susan Flashman/123RF: 29, Shelly Perry/Istockphoto: 31.

Q2AMedia Art Bank: 8.

DAD0043
42010

9 8 7 6 5 4 3 2 1

Contents

Living Dinosaurs

Alligators and crocodiles have been around for millions of years. They were living on Earth at the time of the dinosaurs. But when the dinosaurs died out, these **reptiles** survived! The alligators and crocodiles living today look very similar to their ancient ancestors.

Scaly-skinned Reptiles

Alligators and crocodiles are the largest of the reptiles. They have four legs and a long tail. Their body is covered with a tough, scaly skin. They lay eggs like birds, but their eggs have a soft, leathery shell. Alligators and crocodiles are called **crocodilians**. There are 23 **species** of crocodilian, including similar-looking reptiles called caimans and gharials.

 Most alligators are found in the southeastern United States. They tend to have a shorter, broader snout than crocodiles.

Tail is half the alligator's length

Largest scales are found along the back

Large mouth with about 80 sharp teeth

Four claws on the hind foot

Five claws on the front foot

Alligator or Crocodile?

It can be difficult to tell the difference between alligators and crocodiles. One way is to look at the jaw. The crocodile's fourth tooth on the lower jaw sticks out (above). The snout is more pointed, too.

Large and Small

The longest ever crocodile lived at the time of the dinosaurs. It was 39 feet (12 m) long—about the length of a medium-sized swimming pool! Today, the largest is the saltwater crocodile that grows up to 23 feet (7 m). The smallest is the dwarf crocodile at just 6 feet (1.9 m).

DINOSAUR TERROR

About 135 million years ago, animals living in the sea were terrorized by a vicious crocodile. It had the body of a crocodile but a head more like *Tyrannosaurus Rex*. Its name was *Dakosaurus Andiniensis*.

 Dwarf crocodiles are the only crocodiles that leave the water at night to hunt on land.

Body Armor

Alligators and crocodiles are fully protected by an **armor** of tough skin and bones that covers their body from nose to tail. This armor is thick enough to stop sharp arrows and spears.

Scales and Scutes

The thick skin is made from a substance called keratin. This is the stuff that makes your hair and nails strong. It covers pieces of flat bone called scutes. The bones down the back are particularly large and thick for protection. A crocodile's back is tough and bony, but the underside of the body is covered in small, smooth **scales** that don't catch on rocks or undergrowth.

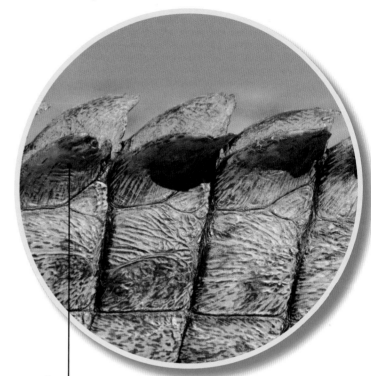

Scales and scutes also reduce the amount of water lost from the skin

These thick scales provide a tough protective armor.

The smooth belly scales slip easily over the ground.

Razor-sharp teeth are good for catching prey and tearing meat.

Growing Teeth

A crocodilian's teeth are a bit like scales. They form from the skin as hollow, cone-shaped teeth without any roots. The mouth is armed with about 80 teeth, and as one falls out, another grows in its place. Over their lifetime, an alligator or crocodile may grow up to 3,000 teeth!

AGING SKIN

It is possible to age an alligator or crocodile by examining its scales. Every year, a growth ring (mark) appears on the scales. You can age the animal by counting the number of rings.

Swampy Homes

Alligators and crocodiles love **swampy** places where there is mud and water. They like it warm too, so they are found mostly in **tropical** and **subtropical** regions, such as Central America and Northern Australia.

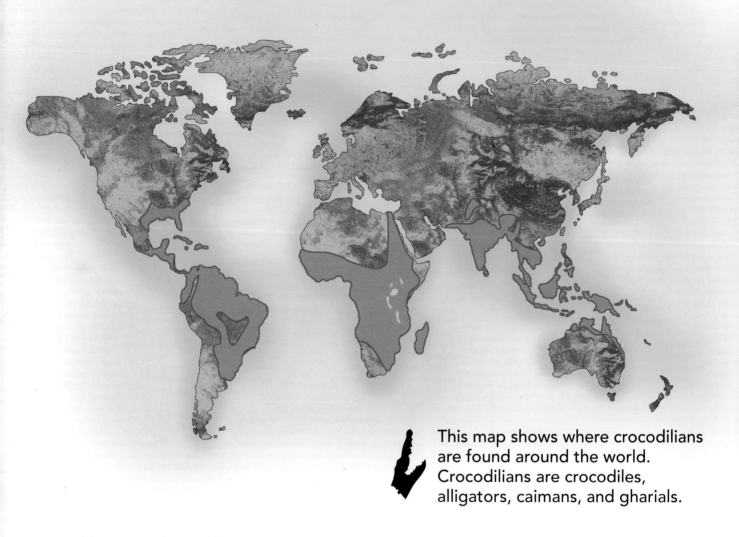

This map shows where crocodilians are found around the world. Crocodilians are crocodiles, alligators, caimans, and gharials.

Crocodile Homes

Crocodiles are found in the southeastern United States, through Central and South America, in Africa, and from India to Australia. One reason for this wide **distribution** is their ability to swim and survive in salt water. Crocodiles have a special salt **gland** on their tongue that gets rid of excess salt. The salt gland allows crocodiles to live along tropical coasts with mangrove swamps, on tropical islands, along rivers, and even in jungles.

 Like other reptiles, a crocodilian's body temperature is similar to its surroundings. Warm, swampy conditions help them to keep active.

Alligator Homes

Alligators are found in far fewer places than crocodiles. The American alligator is found only in the United States, while the Chinese alligator is found in parts of China. Their close relatives, caimans, live mostly in Central and South America.

LIVING TOGETHER

Florida is home to both the alligator and the American crocodile—the only place where these two animals are found together. This is due to the great variety of **habitats**—both salty and fresh water—and the tropical temperatures. American crocodiles can cope with more salt, so they are found in mangrove swamps and saltwater creeks, while alligators prefer freshwater pools and creeks.

King of the Everglades

When the Spanish first arrived in Florida, during the sixteenth century, they found alligators living in the swamps. They called them *el lagarto*, which means lizard, and over time this name changed to "alligator."

Clever Camouflage

American alligators are only found in the southeastern United States, from North Carolina to Texas. These large reptiles grow up to 15 feet (4.5 m) long, and their color varies. If they live in waters with lots of **algae**, they take on a green appearance. Those living in muddier waters under trees are darker. This helps to **camouflage** them in their surroundings.

 This alligator blends in with a log as it suns itself to keep warm.

Storing Water

During the dry months, the water levels fall, and some swamps dry up. The alligators make deep holes in the mud to collect water. These "gator holes" are valuable sources of water for other animals, too.

A racoon is just a medium-sized meal for an alligator. Some attack prey as large as bears.

Large Prey

Alligators are not fussy about their food. Some of the biggest alligators attack large **prey**, such as black bears, pythons, and even panthers. Most years, one or two people are killed by an alligator in the United States, usually when swimming. But alligators rarely attack people, unless they are disturbed, or their young are threatened.

Success Story

The American alligator was once hunted for its skin, which was used to make leather bags and shoes. These creatures almost disappeared, but fortunately, the U.S. government acted to protect them. Since the 1970s, the number of alligators has increased, and now there are more than one million in the wild, and many more in alligator farms.

On the Move

Alligators and crocodiles look like lazy creatures that enjoy floating in water or lying in the sun. But beware—they move surprisingly quickly when they have to!

Surging through Water

Crocodilians are powerful swimmers. Their long tail propels them through the water at speeds of up to 12 miles (20 km) per hour. When they swim quickly, they hold their legs tight against their body, to create a smooth shape that slips easily through the water. They stick their legs out to turn or brake. To dive, crocodiles and alligators breathe out to empty their lungs, and sink down. They use their legs to walk over rocks at the bottom of a river or pool.

Tail pushes body through the water

At slow speeds, only the tail moves from side to side. At higher speeds, the whole body moves, with the legs tucked in.

Legs are tucked in so water flows easily over the body

Legs are straightened to raise body right off the ground

 When walking, alligators and crocodiles can reach speeds of up to 3 miles (5 km) per hour.

The High Walk

Alligators and crocodiles can move quickly on land, too. Mostly, they belly crawl, using their legs to push their bulky body along. Sometimes, they do a "high walk." They straighten their legs and lift their body weight off the ground. This allows them to cross rough ground and clamber over wood and rocks. Some crocodilians gallop over the ground at speeds of up to 11 miles (17 km) per hour before they collapse. This looks a bit like a hopping rabbit, with both hind legs coming forwards together.

EXHAUSTED ALLIGATORS

Alligators soon tire after activity, so they lie around for hours, moving in and out of the shade to keep their body temperature at the right level.

Surprise Attack!

Alligators and crocodiles take their prey by surprise. They lie underwater with just their ears, eyes, and the tip of their snout above the water while they wait for unsuspecting prey to come within reach.

Powerful Bite

These crafty creatures attack without warning, launching themselves from the water with a thrash of their tail. As they open their mouth, they grip their victim between their many teeth. The muscles that clamp the jaws together are so powerful that the teeth can crush a turtle shell.

 An alligator lies waiting for prey to pass by.

When researchers move an alligator or crocodile, the jaws are tied for safety.

Death by Drowning

With a firm grip on their prey, the alligator or crocodile dives under the water where it stays until the animal **drowns**. Alligators and crocodiles can swim underwater with their mouth open because a flap of skin at the back of their mouth closes the opening to their throat. But they have to come to the surface to swallow. They either stick their head above water or drag their prey onto land for their feast.

This gazelle has been caught in the jaws of a hungry crocodile.

SNAPPING JAWS

Powerful muscles shut the jaws of an alligator or crocodile, but the muscles that open them are surprisingly weak. In fact, you could keep an alligator's jaws closed with just an elastic band!

Time to Feast

As predators, crocodiles and alligators feed on many different types of animals. Small crocodiles feed on frogs, fish, snails, and insects, while larger ones catch turtles, fish, small mammals, and birds.

Smaller Portions

A crocodilian's teeth grip and crush their prey, but do not slice it up. Instead, alligators and crocodiles swallow small animals whole. If the animal is too large to swallow, they tear it into smaller pieces. They do this by shaking and twisting their head, so that bits come off. Sometimes, they do a "death roll." They push one end of the prey's body under a rock or log and, while hanging on to the other end, roll in the water to twist a tasty piece off.

 A "death roll" helps to break up large prey, such as zebra.

Acid Stomach

Alligators and crocodiles deliberately swallow stones that collect in their stomach. The stones help to grind up food so that it can be easily digested (broken down). Strong stomach acids also help to digest flesh and bone. The stomach of an alligator has been found to contain nails, glass, and bottle caps, but these cannot be digested.

A twisting crocodile can break the backbone of its prey.

A crocodile may eat up to half its weight in just one meal.

The Nile Crocodile

The Nile crocodile feeds mostly on fish, but attacks anything that ventures near the water. Sometimes, a group of crocodiles work together to catch their prey.

African Giants

Nile crocodiles are the largest crocodiles in Africa. They grow to 16 feet (5 m) in length and weigh up to 1.1 tons (1,000 kg). They live along rivers and lakes, and in freshwater swamps. In summer, they dig burrows in riverbanks to escape the heat.

This crocodile has pounced on a tasty meal as wildebeest cross the Mara River in East Africa.

Guarding Nests

Nile crocodiles live alone for much of the year, but they gather together during the breeding season. Unlike other crocodiles, the female buries her eggs in sand and guards them for three months. When the young crocodiles hatch, she digs them out and carries them to water. The young crocodiles stay close to the female for up to two years until they are ready to fend for themselves.

Nile crocodiles gather together on riverbanks during the breeding season.

Crocodile God

In ancient Egypt, crocodiles were found along the Nile River. Many people working on or near the river were attacked. The crocodile was feared, but also worshipped because it was a strong, fearless animal. Some crocodiles were kept in temples. There are even records of the ancient Egyptians keeping crocodiles in water-filled ditches around important forts and settlements as protection against invaders.

This carving of a crocodile god was found on the walls of an old temple in Egypt.

Sounds and Signals

Early explorers in North America were terrified by roaring and bellowing sounds coming from the swamps. These were the sounds of alligators talking to each other.

Chirps, Roars, and Bellows

Alligators and crocodiles communicate using their senses of sound, smell, and touch, as well as other forms of behavior. The babies chirp in the egg when they are about to hatch, so their mother can find them. Youngsters that are lost or in danger produce a distress call that brings the adults running. Adult crocodiles often roar when they are approached by another adult. Alligators and crocodiles also warn that they are about to attack by thrashing their tail from side to side.

 Male alligators make loud bellowing sounds during the breeding season to attract females.

Showing Off

The largest male in a group is usually the "top" male. He shows off by swimming at the surface, so that all the others can see the length of his body. A smaller male swims deeper in the water, so just his head shows. Sometimes, the top males slap their heads against the water to make a noise, or they breathe out underwater to produce a noisy stream of bubbles.

The sounds this baby alligator makes as it hatches will help its mother find it.

POPPING SOUNDS

Male gharials have a "pot" at the end of their long, thin snout, which they use to make a popping sound to warn off rivals.

Life Story

Spring is a noisy time in the Florida swamps —this is the breeding season of the alligator. The males bellow to warn off other males and to attract the females.

Warm Nest

After mating, the female builds a huge mound of grass, twigs, and soil, in which she lays up to 50 eggs. The mound is like a mini-compost heap. As the vegetation rots, it releases heat that keeps the eggs warm. She guards her nest for about 60 days. The chirps from the eggs tell her to dig out her young and carry them to water.

An alligator searches her nest for her hatching babies.

When baby alligators hatch, they are as small as a human hand.

Staying Together

The youngsters stay together in a group with the female for about a year. They feed on small animals, such as insects, shrimp, frogs, and small fish. Unfortunately, these tiny alligators are preyed upon by other animals. Nine out of ten alligators will die in their first year. As they get older, they get larger and are safer from attacks. An alligator lives for about 35 to 50 years in the wild. They are ready to breed when they are about 10 years old.

BOY OR GIRL?

The sex of a baby alligator depends on the temperature of the nest. More girls are born when the temperature in the nest is under 86°F (30°C), and more boys hatch when the temperature exceeds 93°F (34°C).

Under Threat

Around the world, many types of alligator and crocodile are becoming rarer, and some are even at risk of becoming **extinct**. We need to act now to prevent these important species from dying out.

Hunted Animal

Large crocodilians are dangerous animals and have been killed by people who fear them. But most are hunted for the smooth skin on their belly. Crocodilians are often killed at night because they are easy to find in the dark—their eyes shine in the beam of a searchlight like two red dots. This makes it easy to spear them between the eyes.

Tourist Trail

The American alligator and the saltwater crocodile have been saved by hunting bans. Their numbers have increased, and now many tourists travel to see them. However, other species are still at risk, and more **conservation** is needed.

 Crocodile skin has been used to make leather bags and shoes.

Tourists bring money into an area, which pays for the upkeep of nature reserves.

THE CHINESE ALLIGATOR

There are fewer than 200 Chinese alligators left in the wild. Their homes, in swamps and ponds beside the Yangtze River in China, have been turned into farmland. Fortunately, more than 10,000 Chinese alligators live in zoos and alligator farms, and these creatures could be reintroduced to the wild in the future.

Saltwater Giant

The world's largest crocodile is the saltwater crocodile, or "salty," as it is called in Australia. Once there were millions of saltwater crocodiles, from India to Australia, but hunting has put this species at risk.

Valuable Skin

The salty tops the charts for the number of people it attacks each year, so it is not surprising that people kill it because they are afraid. But saltwater crocodiles are mostly hunted for their particularly soft skin—the most valuable skin of all the crocodilians. Uncontrolled hunting between 1945 and the 1970s led to millions being killed. Today, some illegal hunting still continues in Southeast Asia.

Some saltwater crocodiles are still hunted for their valuable skin.

International Control

When their numbers began to fall, countries such as Australia introduced a hunting ban, and there were international controls on the sale of crocodile skin. Since the 1970s, numbers in Australia have risen to about 300,000 saltwater crocodiles. However, saltwater crocodiles are still at risk elsewhere, especially in India, Thailand, and Indonesia where few survive. This is due to the loss of crocodile habitat and illegal hunting.

Farm Protection

In some places, saltwater crocodiles are raised in special farms for their skin. Surprisingly, this helps to protect the wild crocodiles, too. Crocodile eggs are collected from nests in the wild, and the hatchlings are sold to crocodile farms. The money from the sales goes toward crocodile conservation. In India and Papua New Guinea, crocodiles have now been reintroduced to the wild with some success.

 This crocodile is being raised in a crocodile farm in Malaysia, and may return to the wild.

Facts and Records

The largest of all the reptiles, alligators and crocodiles are feared around the world. They use their size and strength to kill their prey, but they are caring parents, too.

Largest and Smallest

- The largest crocodile is the saltwater crocodile, which grows to 23 feet (7 m).

- The smallest is the dwarf crocodile at 6 feet (1.9 m).

- The largest alligator is the American alligator which grows up to 15 feet (4.5 m).

- The largest ever crocodile lived about 110 million years ago. It was 39 feet (12 m) long and eight times heavier than the saltwater crocodiles living today.

Crocodile Tears

Legend has it that crocodiles cry when they eat humans. When a crocodile eats, its eyes froth slightly. Crocodiles huff and puff when they eat, and scientists think this pushes air into their tear ducts, producing more tears. This may explain the story of the crying crocodile.

The saltwater crocodile is the largest of all.

Body Facts

- When an alligator or crocodile lies completely under the water, its ears are covered by tiny flaps, and its nostrils close to keep out water.

- Alligators and crocodiles have a third transparent eyelid. This protects the eye when the reptile is underwater.

- At the back of the eye of an alligator or crocodile is a special reflective layer, called the tapetum, which gives them excellent night vision. It is this layer that makes their eyes appear red when they are caught in the beam of a searchlight.

Names and Numbers

- The Mugger crocodile gets its name from the Hindi word *magar*, which means "water monster." Muggers live in swamps in South Asia.

- Alligators and crocodiles live for about 50 years, but some crocodiles have been known to live as long as 130 years.

- During the 1950s, as many as 10 million Nile crocodiles were killed each year for their skin.

Did You Know?

- Crocodiles sweat through their mouth. If you spot a crocodile lying with its mouth wide open, it is not being aggressive, it's just cooling off!

- A Nile crocodile called Gustave was believed to have killed up to 300 people during the 1990s. This man-eating crocodile was never caught, but its story was the basis for the movie *Primeval*.

This crocodile looks threatening, but it is just keeping cool!

Glossary

algae
simple plants, often single-celled, that live in water or damp places

armor
protective covering over the body, such as the scutes of a crocodile

camouflage
the colors and patterns on an animal's skin, fur, or feathers that help it blend with its surroundings so that it is hard to see

conservation
the protection of natural habitats, plants, and animals

crocodilian
name given to crocodiles, alligators, and other reptiles, such as caimans and gharials

distribution
the geographic area in which an animal is found around the world

drown
to die in water when water rushes into the lungs

extinct
no longer in existence, having died out

gland
an organ in the body that releases a particular substance, for example, the salivary glands in the mouth release saliva

habitat
a particular place where plants and animals live, such as a swamp

mammal
an animal that feeds its young on milk, and has hair on its body

predator
an animal that hunts others for food

prey
an animal that is eaten for food by another

reptile
a group of vertebrates (animals with a backbone) that usually have a scaly skin, four legs, a tail, and lay eggs

scales
overlapping plates that protect the skin of fish and reptiles

species
a particular type of animal, such as a crocodile

subtropical
an area or climate that is warm, lying to the north and south of the tropical areas

swamp
a low-lying area of wetland with trees and pools of water

tropical
an area or climate that is warm and often wet, close to the equator (the imaginary line around the Earth's middle)

Index

Web Finder

Florida Museum of Natural History—Crocodilians
www.flmnh.ufl.edu/natsci/herpetology/brittoncrocs/cnhc.html
Learn about the 23 species of crocodilians and listen to their calls.

National Geographic—Reptiles
http://animals.nationalgeographic.com/animals/reptiles
Find out about reptiles and what makes them different from other animals.

San Diego Zoo—Alligators and Crocodiles
www.sandiegozoo.org/animalbytes/t-crocodile.html
Facts on crocodiles, alligators, and gharials

National Zoological Park—Reptiles and Amphibians
http://nationalzoo.si.edu/Animals/ReptilesAmphibians/ForKids/default.cfm
Fun facts, animals to color, jigsaw puzzles, and the story behind some reptile names

National Biological Information Infrastructure—Reptiles for Kids
www.nbii.gov/portal/community/Communities/Plants,_Animals_&_Other_Organisms/Reptiles/Reptiles_for_Kids
Information on all kinds of reptiles, stories in the news, photographs, and fun facts